Barkey
The Lost Dog

By Vanella C. Taylor

To order additional copies of this book, contact:
Xlibris
844-714-8691
www.Xlibris.com
Orders@Xlibris.com

ISBN: Softcover   978-1-4535-7178-1
        EBook   978-1-4771-7418-0

Print information available on the last page

Rev. date: 10/24/2023

Acknowledgement

I extend the credit of my inspiration
to be creative in writing to my sister Barbara Ann Yarbrough
1939-2002.

Barkey lives in the house on the corner of the first street in the neighborhood, the street is called Park lane.

Barkey is a beautiful rust colored chow puppy. He is very lucky because he was rescued from an animal shelter by a couple who wanted to share their love with a puppy who needed to be taken care of. Barkey was found abandon by the side of a road and was brought to the shelter. He now lives with Mr. and Mrs. Clark.

Mr. and Mrs. Clark are much older than the other families in the neighborhood.

Barkey has a big doghouse that's usually empty because he spends most of his time inside his best friend's house.

Rob is Barkey's best friend. He is an eight-year-old boy who lives with his mother and does not have a brother or sister. He is in third grade and lives two houses down the street from Barkey.

Mr and Mrs Clark have no children of their own but all the children in the neighborhood love to come by and say hi to Mr. Clark when he is in the yard with Barkey. Mr. Clark feeds Barkey, then takes him for a walk in the morning around the neighborhood, he then returns and works on his model airplane in the garage.

Children come out and watch as Mr. Clark attempts to fly his model airplane. When the plane takes off and flies the entire group of children cheers hooray.

While the children are in the yard, Barkey gets a drink of water after running around the yard playfully chasing birds, rabbits, squirrels and anything else that moves in the yard.

The neighborhood is on the edge of a wooded area where there is a small lake surrounded by trees and wild flowers. Lots of people set up camping around the lake in the spring to fish, cook out and play games, while children are on spring break.

One bright sunny day Rob came running by Mr. Clark's house with his kite high in the sky; the wind was blowing really strong.

When Barkey saw Rob running with the kite he came running behind him; Rob was excited to see that Barkey joined him. He reached over and patted him on his back and the two ran faster and faster until they were out of sight. They ran with the kite until the wind stopped blowing and the kite came slowly, slowly down to the ground.

Rob knew that it was really against the rules to play at or near the lake unless he was with an adult but as he got closer to the lake he could see all the excitement; there were tents, campers and boats. Children were playing hula hoops, hide and seek, throwing balls, roasting marshmallows and fishing.

When they saw Rob and Barkey they came over and greeted them because Barkey was such a big beautiful dog with a great personality. He loved to play and roll over and bark playfully at the children. It didn't take long for Rob to forget the rules when they started running and playing with other children.

Time passed and Rob's mom came outside and called for him to come inside to pick up his toys and get ready for lunch. She made his favorite lunch, fish sticks, potato wedges, broccoli and sliced peaches for dessert. He was out of school and she always made sure he ate a nutritious meal.

She called and called but Rob did not answer her call. She walked out to the edge of the street and checked the back yard, she looked up the street and down the street but there was no Rob in sight.

She walked over to Mr. Clark's house and asked if Rob was there; they said no but he came by earlier with his kite and he and Barkey ran down the street flying the kite together.

Rob's mom returned to her yard to think about where he could be; maybe he is hiding from me.

She walked into his room and looked in his closet but he was not there, she peeked under his bed, he was not there, now she is really concerned, knowing how dangerous some places can be for children.

Rob lived in a quiet suburban neighborhood but his mother knows that bad things sometime happen in good neighborhoods and no child is safe if left alone too long.

Rob and Barkey lost track of time while exploring their surroundings; Rob saw what looked like a tunnel through the trees. He was filled with curiosity, so he decided to follow the trail that led to the tunnel. Walking and throwing rocks at the trees as they came closer to the tunnel.

When they came to the end of the road there was an entrance to the tunnel which led them inside the old mine. Rob did not see the Dangerous Keep Out sign that had fallen off the pole in front of the tunnel.

How exciting to see the inside of a real tunnel. Rob was really curious about the mysterious tunnel; let's go inside Barkey and see what's in there. They went inside of the cold dark tunnel where they could see bats hanging upside down and spiders on the wall.

They could see small rays of sunlight shinning through the broken walls of the tunnel. Rob was fascinated thinking about what might have happened there a long time ago when real people worked there and brought out baskets of black coal that looked shinny and new.

Then there was a cracking sound behind them as they wandered deeper inside the tunnel, by the time Rob said we better get out of here, "because it feels creepy and weird. The floor started falling under them. Rob ran to the edge of the tunnel but Barkey fell through a big crack in the floor of the tunnel and was trapped. Rob yelled for Barkey but all he could hear was a weak bark and then nothing.

Rob called and called for Barkey but all he could hear was a weak bark and then just a whine from Barkey. It sound like Barkey was asking for help. Rob knew that if he tried to reach his friend Barkey, he might get trapped too and no one will know where they were and they might never get out.

Rob called to the dog; saying it's ok, I'll get help, I'll be back Barkey.

Rob ran out of the tunnel and through the trees as fast as his legs could carry him. All he could think about was that his mom said never to go around that lake unless you are with an adult. He did not stop running until he made it to Mr. Clark's house, where his mother and Mr. Clark were standing outside waiting to complete a 911 call to report Rob and Barkey missing.

Rob was out of breath and could only say Barkey, Barkey. His mother told him to calm down and tell them what happened. Then he told them that Barkey was lost in the tunnel by the lake and he couldn't get him out. Mr. Clark grabbed his flashlight, a rope, a shovel and a pick; he and Rob jumped in the truck and went to rescue Barkey.

Rob's mom called her brother Chris who is a fireman, for backup to the rescue. They all arrived at the tunnel and waited for Chris to go in and find Barkey. Chris said to Mr Clark "let me go in first because I know more about safety when attempting a rescue." Rob stayed outside with his mom by the big red fire truck and waited for Barkey to come out.

Chris called Barkey and there was no sound, he called again and there was no sound, when he called the third time and there was no sound from Barkey. He then shined the big flashlight and saw a drop-off in the floor.

Mr. Clark gave a whistle and Barkey barked softly and whined as if he didn't feel much like barking again. Chris followed the sound and shined the light until he found the hole that Barkey fell into. Chris carefully looked into the hole and saw the dog stuck between dirt and rocks.

Chris took a metal clasp and tied it to the rope and reached in and pulled Barkey out.

Barkey was tired and cold but he was not hurt. When Rob saw his best friend he ran to him gave him a big hug and a pat on the back and said we will never leave our street again without permission.

The fireman repaired the sign, put it back in place on the pole and reminded Rob never go inside old caves, tunnels, or mine shafts because they can be very dangerous. Rob and Barkey were glad to be safe again. They went home where there was hot chocolate for Rob and a dog biscuit for Barkey.

Rob's mom gave him a big hug and said I love you so much and am glad you are safe, oh and Barkey too.

Printed in the United States
by Baker & Taylor Publisher Services